The Persistent Trillium

poems by

Brenda Kay Ledford

Finishing Line Press
Georgetown, Kentucky

The Persistent Trillium

ACKNOWLEDGMENTS

These poems first appeared in the following publications:

"The Music of Maples," *Whispering Willow Tree Poems*
"The Rock," *Fresh Literary Magazine*
"Ambidextrous," *Wild Goose Poetry Review*
"Snowstorm," *The Aurorean*
"Pursuing Freedom," *Immigration Emigration Diversity*
"Invasion," *Poets for Peace*

Publisher: Leah Huete de Maines
Editor: Christen Kincaid
Cover Art: Barbara Ledford Wright
Author Photo: Barbara Ledford Wright
Cover Design: Elizabeth Maines McCleavy

Order online: www.finishinglinepress.com
                also available on amazon.com

Author inquiries and mail orders:
Finishing Line Press
PO Box 1626
Georgetown, Kentucky 40324
USA

Contents

The Rock

fter Mary Oliver's "The Summer Day"

What if this rock could talk?
What would it tell me?
Would it scream with pain
when tires, toys, or trains
run over her bones?
This rock, the one thrown
into the stream, would
she gaze with wild eyes,
snap her jaws like a turtle,
or lift her arms and wash
her face, then float away?
I don't know how a rock
feels when cast aside,
or ground into gravel.
I can only pick up a rock,
hold it to the light,
and wish it were a ring.
Does everything feel pain?
Tell me, can a heart of stone
become a living flesh?

Snowstorm

Flat-faced searching
   in the darkness of winter
      over fractured ice

Blindfolded by white
   no features to guide
      across crystal asparagus

I join the rookery
   dress in Tuxedo glide
      toboggan style
         on my belly

Flat-faced no direction
   part of the emperor band
      forming a V-shape

Going through the motions
   bland as an egg white
      absorbed in the journey

Flat-faced searching
   trail fading in snowfall
      I take the fork
         to freedom

Ambidextrous

Even at six,
I knew I was
meant to be left-handed.

When my teacher
turned her back
to help other students

in the first grade,
I held my pencil
in the left hand.

Minutes ticked like hours
on the classroom clock,
the teacher caught me

and slapped the defiant hand.
I hid my talent,
colored with a chastised fist.

Discards

Rummaging through the trash,
discards make beautiful patterns
stained-glass
imagination
colors
designs
stained-glass
creative
flowing
details
stained-glass
Discards make beautiful patterns
Rummaging through the trash

Broken

For years I dodged
road blocks, skirted around
rockslides and fallen trees.

Like a feisty pup,
I begged for scraps
from the table.

The peacemaker
could not stop
the oozing wounds.

Artificial relationships
soon crack as eggs.
You can't draw water

from a dry well,
money can't heal
a broken heart.

Suffering

Some people snap
like the Gympie Gympie,
the stinging tree.

They see a victim
and inflict unbearable
pain as hot acid

and electrocution together.
You suffer for years
from the rejection and hate,

trying to mend the wounds,
but the suicide plant
has fulfilled its mission.

Jealousy

Cut through the ice,
kindness is like melted butter
drizzled on dry ingredients.

Ignore their turned backs,
the frowns when you speak,
exclusion from the inner circle.

Overhearing snide remarks,
sticks and stones may break
the bones, but words hurt.

Flatter the jealous women,
elevate their fragile egos,
I really don't care!

Guilt

The creature crawls
from under the floor,
stands on hind legs,
and points its claws.

Lurking in the dark waters,
he leaps from the rocks,
tries to wrap his arms
like an octopus around me.

Large eyes glare and accuse.
Negative thoughts bombard,
I stand in judgement,
flooded with guilt.

What more could I have done?
I did my best to please:
use caution when handling
an octopus, it bites.

Blunders

When you trip and get
the hoof and mouth disease,
don't back walk as politicians.

You only sink deeper
into the quick sand
trying to correct a blunder.

Claim the senior moment
when you forget names,
or don't say their names.

Change the subject,
ask the person questions,
but don't ever back walk.

Grief

Dance in the sunrays
ricocheting over the mountains,
spring forth as morning glories,
shed the beggar's coat.

Lift your drooping head
as the tiger lilies shrivel,
petals scattered on the wind;
rag weeds choke the garden

that you planted, could not tend.
Clap your hands,
as the poplar trees lifting
their palms to azure skies.

Shed the beggar's coat.
A new day is rising,
the river of life skips
over the rocks, sing a song!

Screenwriting

This script is finished
I cannot remake
the motion picture

Guilt and self-condemnation
cannot change
any of the scenes

The midpoint turn
could not reverse
a spiral dissension

to the third act
the inevitable ending
of her long life

Child Labor

Mother Jones was mad
as a hornet at bad bosses
making dirty, ragged, starving
kids work ten hours a day

in the hot, filthy factories.
The rich got richer,
abusing the poor children.
Mother Jones led a protest march.

The kids fighting for freedom,
they slept in barns,
camped under the stars,
marching a hundred miles.

Exhausted in the summer heat,
bound for New York City.
They paraded up Fourth Avenue,
helped to pass child labor laws.

Balto

Throughout the ages epidemics
have burst forth, swept the earth
as a wildfire burning
a forest to ashes.

The deadly disease of diphtheria
struck Nome, Alaska in 1925.
A telegram was sent
for one million units of serum.

Cut off by snowstorms,
too dangerous to fly.
Panic. Would stricken people die?
Could dogs carry the medicine?

Balto led the sled team
through the Arctic blizzards,
across the treacherous waters,
lost some of the dogs.

The heroic husky saved the team.
Fans erected a statue
in New York City's Central Park
dedicated to his endurance.

Pursuing Freedom

Haitians,
hunger, horror,
fear of persecution,
crossing the ocean,
rickety, wooden boats,
sharks, storms,
waves churning,
diseases, deaths,
dodging the Cost Guard,
dry land,
passing children to the shore
like potato sacks,
a rush for freedom.

Invasion

Far away from the world,
a hush fills the hills,
the temple beneath silken skies
where I find peace in the storm.

Fields swell with goldenrod
and dogwoods wear crosses,
a shadow on scorched grass.

Poplar leaves rustle
in the rasping wind.
Warning posted on the coast:
a mean season for hurricanes.

Global warming, school violence,
fires raging, bombs and wars,
guns take innocent lives:
peace flees into the night.

Violets

The tropical plants graced
our red-plank house.
White, pink, and violet:
love on a lace-covered table.

Heart-shaped fuzzy leaves,
Hardy, surviving for years,
they were birthday gifts
from my former students.

Mama pitched the leaves
and rooted the violets
in a glass of water.
they symbolized strength

and beauty in winter.
The blue hues sparkled
joy in the sickroom,
mood boosters when bedridden.

Trillium

The trillium dance
in pink slippers
through the woods
and over the pine needles.

These fairies dance
in pink gowns
and twirl pink streamers
for a mountain ball.

They dance all day,
their musicians are
the bullfrogs that blow
trumpets on the pond.

Above their heads
is a tent of cobalt skies,
white-tailed deer pluck
wild strawberries from vines.

Leatherwood Falls

Like a wrinkle between mountains,
the gorge in crescendo resounds:
a thunderstorm with cloudless sky.

Off the wilderness trail,
spice bush, poplar, black gum, border
Fires Creek that slices

through the S-shaped trough
and blocks all worry;
stress, fear, woe, seem

far away. A water thrush cuts
above the virgin forest
where horses clop over

rocks, tree roots, briars:
scraping flanks, they ascend
the leaf-quilted hill.

Snorting, they stumble
with the riders and heave
over the ridge reaching
a crashing waterfall.

The Music of Maples

We are the trees
rocking baby bluebirds
to sleep in our arms.

We are the trees
cooling the skin
of children playing.

We are the trees
singing melodies each night
through the open windows.

We are the trees
that wear rubies each fall
reflecting like fire on rivers.

We are the trees
who breathe into the lungs
and give life to Mother Earth.

Brenda Kay Ledford is a member of North Carolina Writers' Network and listed with "A Directory of American Poets and Fiction Writers." Her work has appeared in many journals including *Asheville Poetry Review, Pembroke Magazine, Appalachian Heritage*, 49 Old Mountain Press anthologies, and other publications.

Ledford has received the Paul Green Multimedia Award thirteen times from North Carolina Society of Historians for her blogs, books, and collecting oral history on Southern Appalachia. She's the author of *Red Plank House, Reagan's Romps, Sacred Fire, Beckoning, The Singing Convention, Blanche, Poems of a Blue Ridge Woman.*